Published 2011
First published in hardback 2010 by
A&C Black Publishers Ltd.
36 Soho Square, London, W1D 3QY

www.acblack.com

ISBN 978-1-4081-2684-4

Series consultant: Gill Matthews

Text copyright © 2010 Angela Royston

The right of Angela Royston to be identified as the author of this work has been asserted by her in accordance with the Copyrights, Designs and Patents Act 1988.

A CIP catalogue for this book is available from the British Library.

Every effort has been made to trace copyright holders and to obtain their permission for use of copyright material. The author and publishers would be pleased to rectify any error or omission in future editions.

This book is produced using paper that is made from wood grown in managed, sustainable forests. It is natural, renewable and recyclable. The logging and manufacturing processes conform to the environmental regulations of the country of origin.

Produced for A&C Black by Calcium. www.calciumcreative.co.uk

Printed and bound in China by C&C Offset Printing Co.

All the internet addresses given in this book were correct at the time of going to press. The author and publishers regret any inconvenience caused if addresses have changed or sites have ceased to exist, but can accept no responsibility for any such changes.

Acknowledgements

The publishers would like to thank the following for their kind permission to reproduce their photographs:

Cover: Corbis: tr, Hulton-Deutsch Collection br; Shutterstock. **Pages:** Alamy Images: Pictorial Press Ltd 24; Apple: 27b; Corbis: Ted Soqui 26; Fotolia: Comugnero Silvana 23r; Getty Images: The Bridgeman Art Library/John Seymour Lucas 8; Istockphoto: Kkgas 23l, Marco Maccarini 19b, Chris Price 15t, Duncan Walker 9; Library of Congress: 14, 20l, 20r, 21, Detroit Publishing Company Photograph Collection 15b, Raff & Gammon 13; Photolibrary: North Wind Picture Archives 7; Rex Features: Roger-Viollet 6; Shutterstock: Adisa 5, Robert Hardholt 27t, Denis Klimov 25b, Emin Kuliyev 11b, Margot Petrowski 29; U.S. Air Force: 25t; Wikimedia Commons: 4, 10, 11t, 12t, 12b, 16, 22, Maryland Newspaper Project 19t, Smithsonian Institution Libraries 18, Zenodot Verlagsgesellschaft mbH 17l, 17r; Wikipedia: Enrique Dans 28.

CONTENTS

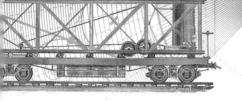

A SPARK OF GENIUS

An invention is a machine or **device** that changes the way something is done. Most inventions change things a little bit at a time, but sometimes, a single invention can change people's lives.

'Genius is one per cent inspiration and ninety-nine per cent perspiration.'

Thomas Edison

Changing the world

For thousands of years people lived in villages, travelled on foot or by horse, and made things in small workshops. Today most people live in cities and travel by car, train, and aeroplane. They have computers and many other electrical gadgets made in large factories. These huge changes are the result of just a few inventions.

▼ Until the nineteenth century most people walked from place to place. Only a few people travelled in horse-drawn carriages.

▲ *Today, wide streets are crowded with cars, motorbikes, and buses.*

Solving problems

Inventors may not set out to change the world. James Watt (see page 6) was simply trying to make an existing steam engine work better. Guglielmo Marconi (see page 18) used the work of other scientists to invent a way of sending and receiving radio signals. He had no idea that his invention would lead to television and mobile phones!

WHAT DOES IT TAKE?
Inventors often have the ability to see things in a different way and so hit on a totally new solution. To other people this looks like a spark of genius.

JAMES WATT

< <   T I M E L I N E   > >

- **1736**   Born on 19 January in Greenock, Scotland
- **1765**   Invented a successful steam engine
- **1819**   Died on 19 August

'I can think of nothing but this engine.'

James Watt

Watt's steam engine was used in factories, trains, and ships. It changed the way people worked and travelled.

▼ *James Watt*

James Watt enjoyed mathematics at school, and his father taught him **carpentry**. He trained as an instrument-maker and found work at Glasgow University.

Inventing a new engine

In 1763 the university asked him why the steam engines that were used in coal mines needed so much steam. The answer came to Watt quite suddenly, when he was out walking one Sunday in May 1765. He designed a new engine in his head, and next day made a small **model** of it. It used much less steam than the existing engine.

Success

Watt then made a full-size engine, but it kept leaking steam. It took him nine years to solve these problems. By then, he had formed a company with Matthew Boulton. In 1776, the first Boulton–Watt engine was installed in a coal mine. It worked brilliantly! Boulton then encouraged Watt to adapt his engine so that it could turn factory machines.

RICH AND FAMOUS
By 1800, 84 cotton mills were using Watt's new engine to turn cotton into fabric. Watt became famous and wealthy.

▼ *Factories using Watt's steam engines were built across Britain.*

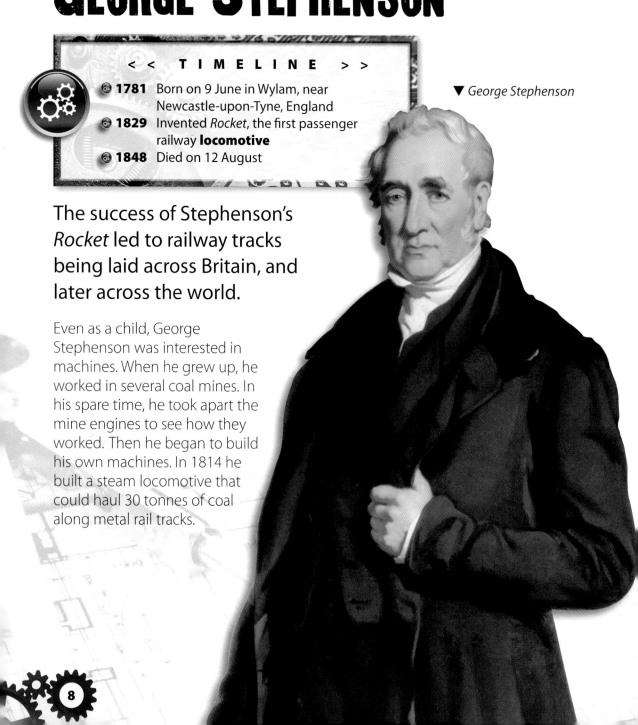

GEORGE STEPHENSON

< < T I M E L I N E > >

- **1781** Born on 9 June in Wylam, near Newcastle-upon-Tyne, England
- **1829** Invented *Rocket*, the first passenger railway **locomotive**
- **1848** Died on 12 August

▼ *George Stephenson*

The success of Stephenson's *Rocket* led to railway tracks being laid across Britain, and later across the world.

Even as a child, George Stephenson was interested in machines. When he grew up, he worked in several coal mines. In his spare time, he took apart the mine engines to see how they worked. Then he began to build his own machines. In 1814 he built a steam locomotive that could haul 30 tonnes of coal along metal rail tracks.

Locomotion

George formed a company with his son Robert and built a faster locomotive called *Locomotion*. In 1825 *Locomotion* was used to haul coal on a new railway line between Stockton and the port of Darlington.

'By the time the [train] arrived at Stockton, where it was received with great joy, there were not less than 600 persons within, and hanging by the carriages.'

John Sykes, who watched the opening of the Stockton to Darlington Railway

ROCKETING TO SUCCESS

In 1829 a competition called the Rainhill Trials was held to choose a locomotive to pull passenger trains between Liverpool and Manchester. Stephenson entered *Rocket*, a new locomotive, and it won the competition!

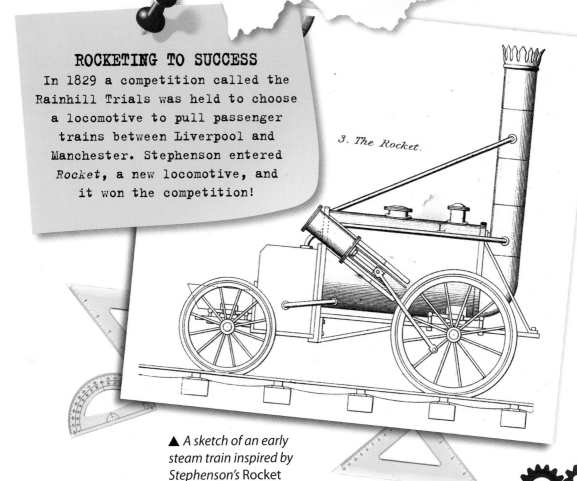

3. The Rocket.

▲ *A sketch of an early steam train inspired by Stephenson's* Rocket

MICHAEL FARADAY

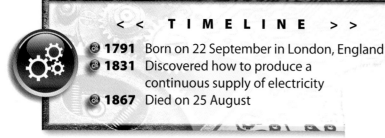

< < T I M E L I N E > >

- **1791** Born on 22 September in London, England
- **1831** Discovered how to produce a continuous supply of electricity
- **1867** Died on 25 August

'Nothing is too wonderful to be true if it be consistent with the laws of nature.'

Michael Faraday

Faraday invented an electric **generator** and an **electric motor**. All the electrical equipment we plug in and use today followed on from his work.

◀ *Michael Faraday*

Michael Faraday's father was a **blacksmith** and Faraday was poorly educated. When he was 14, however, he became an **apprentice** to a **bookbinder**. Faraday loved reading and he educated himself by reading the books he bound, particularly the science books.

▲ Humphry Davy

Help from Humphry

In 1812 Faraday began to attend lectures given by the famous scientist Humphry Davy. When Davy's eyesight was damaged in an accident, he employed Faraday as his secretary and scientific assistant. In 1815, Davy recommended Faraday for a job at the **Royal Institution**.

MOTORS AND GENERATORS

While Faraday was helping Davy, he began his own investigations. He showed that it is possible to **generate** electricity by moving a magnet inside a coil of wire. From this, Faraday invented an electric motor and a generator, which together made electricity into a powerful source of energy.

▼ Today, we use electricity for lighting and to run many machines.

THOMAS ALVA EDISON

< < T I M E L I N E > >

- **1847** Born on 11 February in Ohio, United States
- **1876** Set up an "inventions laboratory" which resulted in more than 1,000 inventions
- **1931** Died 18 October

▼ *An exhausted Edison and his phonograph in 1888*

Edison's inventions included many things that we now take for granted, such as electric lighting.

Thomas Edison was a curious and lively child. He was too lively to fit in at school, so his mother taught him at home. He was always eager to try new experiments to see what would happen.

◄ *Thomas Alva Edison as a boy*

Inventive mind

When he grew up, Edison had so many ideas for inventions that he set up an inventions factory at Menlo Park in New Jersey, where he then lived. The most famous invention that he developed at Menlo Park was the electric light. He not only invented a successful light bulb, he designed everything else that was needed, from light switches to electricity **meters**.

EDISON THE SHOWMAN

Edison laid electric cables to one area in New York. To **publicize** his inventions, he invited important people to a grand opening. They all waited in the dark until, when the electricity began to flow, the whole area slowly lit up. Edison's fame spread around the world.

▲ Edison's kinetoscope was an early movie projector.

'Many of life's failures are people who did not realize how close they were to success when they gave up.'

Thomas Edison

ALEXANDER GRAHAM BELL

< < **T I M E L I N E** > >

- **1847** Born on 3 March in Edinburgh, Scotland
- **1876** Invented the telephone
- **1922** Died on 2 August

Telephones allowed people to communicate instantly, even though they were far apart.

'Writing ... is a slow and tedious way of expressing myself. I long for one of our old confabulations [chats].'

From a letter written by Alexander Graham Bell to a friend

Bell was always interested in the way the human voice made sounds. As a teenager, he even managed to get the family dog to growl in a way that sounded like speech!

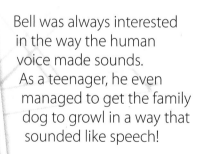

◀ *Alexander Graham Bell*

Moving to Canada

In 1870 the family moved to Canada. Bell was interested in the **telegraph**, which was a way of sending electrical signals along a wire using **Morse code**. Bell, however, wanted to send and receive speech so that he could actually talk to his friends.

▲ *An operator sends and receives messages using Morse code*

Inventing the telephone

The telegraph made signals by turning a current on and off. In 1874 Bell got the idea of changing the strength of the electrical current to be like speech. With the help of Thomas Watson, an **electrical engineer**, he developed his idea. He made a great number of experiments and finally, in March 1876, he succeeded.

▲ *This early telephone has a trumpet for listening to the incoming call.*

PHONES FOR EVERYONE
Bell set up the Bell Telephone Company and began to supply phones to the public.

KARL BENZ

< < T I M E L I N E > >

- **1844** Born on 25 November in Karlsruhe, Germany
- **1885** Invented the first successful motorcar fuelled by petrol
- **1929** Died on 4 April

Motorcars allowed people to travel by road when and where they liked. Cars eventually became the main form of land transport in many countries.

When he was young Karl Benz dreamed of producing a "horseless carriage" – a vehicle that would power itself. He studied **mechanical engineering** at university.

◀ *Karl Benz*

▼ *Several inventors came up with sketches for early cars. This is one of them.*

▲ *The first cars were open to the wind and cold, and they frequently broke down.*

Benz's three-wheeler

In 1883 Benz set up Benz & Company in Mannheim. There he began to develop engines that were powered by burning petrol. He also invented all the mechanical parts that he needed to build his first motorcar, including the gears and a way of starting the engine. He drove his three-wheeled motorcar through Mannheim in 1885, and in 1886 he obtained a **patent** for it.

BERTHA'S FAMOUS DRIVE

Benz's wife Bertha helped to make the car famous. In 1888, she drove it for 106 kilometres (66 miles). There were no petrol stations at that time, but petrol was sold as a cleaning product in chemists' shops. Bertha had to keep stopping to buy more petrol! But she proved that the car could be driven for long distances.

GUGLIELMO MARCONI

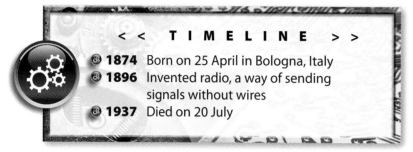

<< **T I M E L I N E** >>

- **1874** Born on 25 April in Bologna, Italy
- **1896** Invented radio, a way of sending signals without wires
- **1937** Died on 20 July

As a child, Guglielmo was always interested in science and so, when he failed to get into university, he decided to study at home. He was fascinated by Heinrich Hertz's discovery that invisible waves could be **transmitted** without wires across a room.

Today radio signals are used to **broadcast** radio and television programmes and to send mobile phone messages around the world.

▼ *Guglielmo Marconi*

Increasing distance

Marconi experimented with these invisible waves, until he was able to transmit and receive signals over 1.5 kilometres (1 mile). Since the Italian government was not interested in his invention, he travelled to London in 1896. Here he got backing and a patent for his "wireless-telegraph".

Over the next few years he sent and received signals over longer and longer distances, until, in 1901, he managed to send a signal right across the Atlantic Ocean!

▲ Many passengers were saved when the liner Titanic sank in 1912, because the ship broadcast radio distress signals.

SPREAD OF RADIO

At first, Marconi's wireless telegraph was used mainly by ships. Later, other scientists discovered how to use radio signals to transmit the human voice, and in the 1920s the first radio stations began broadcasting music for entertainment.

▶ St John's Hill, in Newfoundland, Canada. It was here that the first radio signal to cross the Atlantic was received.

THE WRIGHT BROTHERS

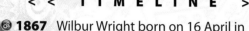

TIMELINE

- **1867** Wilbur Wright born on 16 April in Indiana, United States
- **1871** Orville Wright born on 19 August in Ohio, United States
- **1903** Invented an aeroplane powered by an engine
- **1912** Wilbur died on 30 May
- **1948** Orville died on 30 January

The Wright brothers made the first aeroplane flight. Their work has made it possible for people to fly all over the world.

'If birds can glide for long periods of time, then ... why can't I?'

Orville Wright

▼ *Orville Wright*

▲ *Wilbur Wright*

▲ *Orville Wright's first flight, made at Kitty Hawk in North Carolina, lasted just 12 seconds.*

Even as children the Wright brothers were good at making machines. Later, when they left school, they opened a bicycle shop and sold bicycles they had made themselves.

Experiments with flying

A few people had already flown **gliders**. The Wright brothers experimented to find a way of steering the glider by moving the wings. Then they designed and built an engine.

THE FIRST FLIGHT

By 1903, the Wrights attempted to fly several times and failed. Then, on 17 December, they tried again and this time the plane lifted 6 metres (20 ft) off the ground and flew 37 metres (121 ft). The age of powered flight had arrived!

LEO BAEKELAND

< < **T I M E L I N E** > >

- **1863** Born on 14 November near Ghent, Belgium
- **1907** Developed Bakelite, the first completely **synthetic** plastic
- **1944** Died on 23 February

'It was kind of an accident, because plastic is not what I meant to invent.'

Leo Baekeland

Leo Baekeland's synthetic material led to all the many kinds of plastic that we use today.

Leo Baekeland studied **chemistry** at the University of Ghent, but when he was 26 he moved to New York in the United States. Here he invented a new kind of photographic paper, which he called Velox.

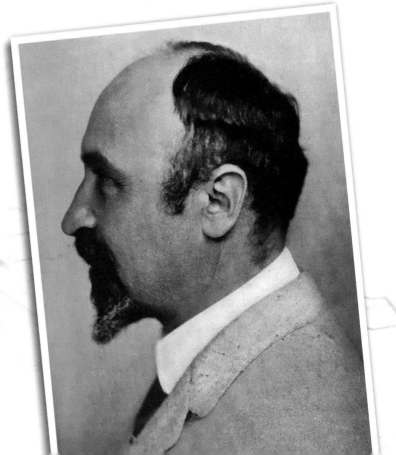

▶ *Leo Baekeland*

Almost a millionaire

In 1898, a photographic company paid Baekeland $750,000 for Velox. The money meant that he never had to work again! Instead he spent his time experimenting with new synthetic materials.

Old Faithful

He heated different substances in a kind of pressure cooker, which he called "Old Faithful". It was while he was trying to find a better way to produce **asbestos** that he discovered a new substance, which he called Bakelite.

BAKELITE

Bakelite could be easily moulded to any shape, so it was made into many different things, from knife handles to telephones. It was particularly useful in making cars and electrical goods. Baekeland became a multimillionaire!

▼ *An early gramophone plays a record made of Bakelite*

▲ *A telephone made of Bakelite*

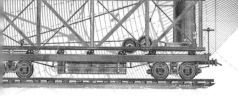

ALAN TURING

< <   T I M E L I N E   > >

- **1912** Born on 23 June in London, England
- **1945–54** Developed much of the basic technology used in computers
- **1954** Died on 7 June

▼ *Alan Turing*

Alan Turing's work paved the way for computers, which have revolutionized the way people work, communicate, and play.

Alan Turing was a mathematical genius. After Turing graduated from Cambridge University he went on to study codes and code-breaking at Princeton University in the United States. He returned to Britain in 1938, just before World War II began.

Secret service

During the war Turing worked as a code-breaker for the British secret service. He built a machine, called "Bombe", which helped to break Enigma, the complex code the Germans used to communicate with their submarines.

First computers

After the war, Turing worked on the design for an Automatic Computing Engine (ACE). His design would have worked, but his **colleagues** were not convinced so he never made it. However, Turing developed much of the science that makes today's computers possible.

▶ *This is a replica of Alan Turing's original Bombe, which could test millions of possible codes very quickly.*

'A computer would deserve to be called intelligent if it could deceive a human into believing that it was human.'

Alan Turing

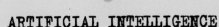

ARTIFICIAL INTELLIGENCE

Turing was also interested in artificial intelligence — that is, a computer that can "think", rather than just carry out instructions. This has still not been achieved.

◀ *Asimo is a modern robot that can do some of the things humans can do.*

MARTIN COOPER

<< TIMELINE >>

- **1928** Born on 26 December in Illinois, United States
- **1973** Invented the first mobile phone

Martin Cooper studied electrical engineering at university before joining the US navy during the Korean War. After the war, he worked at Teletype and then moved to Motorola in 1954.

Mobile phones are changing people's lives around the world. Today mobile phones can access the **Internet**, and take and transmit photographs and videos.

'People want to talk to other people – not a house, or an office, or a car.'

Martin Cooper

◀ *Martin Cooper holding one of the very first mobile phones*

From carphones to mobile phones

In the 1970s, Cooper was put in charge of designing carphones. He wanted to develop a phone that was small enough to be carried around outside a car as well as inside. It took Cooper and his engineers just three months to produce the first model in 1972.

▲ Mobile phones can be used in places where there are no telephone wires.

FIRST CALL

On 3 April 1973, Cooper used his hand-held phone in the street. People were amazed to see him walking down the street speaking on a telephone. Over the next 10 years mobile phones became smaller and lighter. In 1984 the first mobile phones were sold to the public.

▲ Today's mobile phones are mini computers.

TIM BERNERS-LEE

< < TIMELINE > >

- **1955** Born on 8 June in London, England
- **1991** Invented the World Wide Web

'Sites need to be able to interact in one single, universal space.'

Tim Berners-Lee

The World Wide Web makes a vast library of information and file sharing available to everyone.

As a child, Tim Berners-Lee was fascinated by encyclopedias, computers, and how people acquired knowledge. While he was at Oxford University studying physics, he made his own computer, using a television set, a **microprocessor**, and a **soldering iron**.

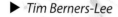

▶ *Tim Berners-Lee*

Sharing information

In the 1980s Berners-Lee was working at **CERN** in Switzerland, when he came up with the idea of linking computers so that people around the world could easily share reports and other information. He called the system "Enquire". Then in 1989 he invented hypertext, a way of linking computers that makes file sharing easy. In 1991, the World Wide Web was made available on the Internet.

NOT RICH OR FAMOUS
Tim Berners-Lee could have made a fortune from his invention, but he chose not to. He was more concerned that the information on the Web was freely available.

▲ *The World Wide Web can be accessed on any computer.*

GLOSSARY

apprentice someone who is learning a skill or craft by working alongside a skilled person

asbestos substance that does not burn

blacksmith person who makes horseshoes and other things made of iron

bookbinder person who binds together the pages and cover of books

broadcast to send a programme or some information using radio or television

carpentry skill of building with wood and repairing things made of wood

CERN European Organization for Nuclear Research's centre for scientific research

chemistry study of the simple substances that combine together to make up all the substances in the world

colleagues people who work together

device something invented for a particular purpose

electric motor engine that is powered by electricity

electrical engineer person who works with electrical machines

generate create or bring into being

gliders lightweight aircrafts with a small motor

generator machine that produces electricity

Internet network that links computers around the world

locomotive engine that pulls wagons and carriages along a railway track

mechanical engineering branch of engineering that deals with machines

meters instruments for measuring something, such as the amount of electricity used

microprocessor tiny piece of silicon that contains many of the programs and processes required by a computer

model small-scale version of something

Morse code code that uses long and short sounds, or dots and dashes, to represent the letters of the alphabet

patent legal document that gives an inventor the right to make and sell a unique invention and stops other people from using the invention without paying for it

perspiration sweat

publicize to make public or tell people about something

Royal Institution organization based in London that encourages research in science

soldering iron tool that uses hot metal to join two pieces of metal

synthetic made from chemicals

telegraph communication by sending electrical signals along an electric wire

transmitted sent

FURTHER INFORMATION

Websites

Read biographies of some of the most famous inventors at:
library.thinkquest.org/5847/halloffame.htm

There are more short biographies of ten famous inventors at:
www.inventorresource.co.uk/TheTopTenGreatestInventors.html

Read a biography of Alexander Graham Bell with links to other websites about him at:
www.alexandergrahambell.org

There is a detailed biography of George Stephenson at:
www.spartacus.schoolnet.co.uk/RAstephensonG.htm

A biography of Guglielmo Marconi can be found at:
nobelprize.org/nobel_prizes/physics/laureates/1909/marconi-bio.html

Read an account of the Wright brothers and their historic first flight at:
www.biographyshelf.com/wright_brothers_biography.html

Books

Inventors and their Bright Ideas (Dead Famous), by Mike Goldsmith. Hippo (2002).

Inventor's Secret Scrapbook, by Chris Oxlade. A&C Black (2010).

Great Inventors and Their Inventions, by David Angus. Naxos Audio Books (2006).

Places to visit

The Science Museum
South Kensington, London
www.science museum.org/uk

INDEX